Acting Edition

I0310425

Theater Masters' Take Ten Volume IX

Below
by Malena Pennycook

big and small
by DJ Hills

de tal palo, tal astilla
by jose sebastian alberdi

ONE HUNDRED BEES
by Katie Kirk

That Was Fun
by Chad Kaydo

‖SAMUEL FRENCH‖

Below © 2024 by Malena Pennycook
big and small © 2024 by DJ Hills
de tal palo, tal astilla © 2024 by jose sebastian alberdi
ONE HUNDRED BEES © 2024 by Katie Kirk
That Was Fun © 2024 by Chad Kaydo
All Rights Reserved

THEATER MASTERS' TAKE TEN VOLUME IX is fully protected under the copyright laws of the United States of America, the British Commonwealth, including Canada, and all member countries of the Berne Convention for the Protection of Literary and Artistic Works, the Universal Copyright Convention, and/or the World Trade Organization conforming to the Agreement on Trade Related Aspects of Intellectual Property Rights. All rights, including professional and amateur stage productions, recitation, lecturing, public reading, motion picture, radio broadcasting, television, online/digital production, and the rights of translation into foreign languages are strictly reserved.

ISBN 978-0-573-71126-8

www.concordtheatricals.com
www.concordtheatricals.co.uk

FOR PRODUCTION INQUIRIES

UNITED STATES AND CANADA
info@concordtheatricals.com
1-866-979-0447

UNITED KINGDOM AND EUROPE
licensing@concordtheatricals.co.uk
020-7054-7298

Each title is subject to availability from Concord Theatricals Corp., depending upon country of performance. Please be aware that *THEATER MASTERS' TAKE TEN VOLUME IX* may not be licensed by Concord Theatricals Corp. in your territory. Professional and amateur producers should contact the nearest Concord Theatricals Corp. office or licensing partner to verify availability.

CAUTION: Professional and amateur producers are hereby warned that *THEATER MASTERS' TAKE TEN VOLUME IX* is subject to a licensing fee. The purchase, renting, lending or use of this book does not constitute a license to perform this title(s), which license must be obtained from Concord Theatricals Corp. prior to any performance. Performance of this title(s) without a license is a violation of federal law and may subject the producer and/or presenter of such performances to civil penalties. Both amateurs and professionals considering a production are strongly advised to apply to the appropriate agent before starting rehearsals, advertising, or booking a theatre. A licensing fee must be paid whether the title(s) is presented for charity or gain and whether or not admission is charged. Professional/Stock licensing fees are quoted upon application to Concord Theatricals Corp.

This work is published by Samuel French, an imprint of Concord Theatricals Corp.

No one shall make any changes in this title(s) for the purpose of production. No part of this book may be reproduced, stored in a retrieval system, scanned, uploaded, or transmitted in any form, by any means, now known or yet to be invented, including mechanical, electronic, digital, photocopying, recording, videotaping, or otherwise, without the prior written permission of the publisher. No one shall share this title(s), or any part of this title(s), through any social media or file hosting websites.

For all inquiries regarding motion picture, television, online/digital and other media rights, please contact Concord Theatricals Corp.

MUSIC AND THIRD-PARTY MATERIALS USE NOTE

Licensees are solely responsible for obtaining formal written permission from copyright owners to use copyrighted music and/or other copyrighted third-party materials (e.g. artworks, logos) in the performance of this play and are strongly cautioned to do so. If no such permission is obtained by the licensee, then the licensee must use only original music and materials that the licensee owns and controls. Licensees are solely responsible and liable for clearances of all third-party copyrighted materials, including without limitation music, and shall indemnify the copyright owners of the play(s) and their licensing agent, Concord Theatricals Corp., against any costs, expenses, losses and liabilities arising from the use of such copyrighted third-party materials by licensees. For music, please contact the appropriate music licensing authority in your territory for the rights to any incidental music.

IMPORTANT BILLING AND CREDIT REQUIREMENTS

If you have obtained performance rights to this title, please refer to your licensing agreement for important billing and credit requirements.

THEATER MASTERS' STAFF & BOARD

Program Director: Emily Zemba
Executive Artistic Director: Victoria Hansen
Artistic Administrator: Lulu Guzman
Founder & Artistic Advisor: Julia Hansen

Board of Directors: Julia Hansen (President), Leyla Bader, Danielle Chock, Victoria Hansen, Gerri Kartesky, Marianne Lubar, Naomi McDougall Jones, Virginia Pearce, Amy Rose Marsh, Jessica Salet, Nancy Stevens, Charlotte Tripplehorn, Daisy Walker

National Advisory Board: Chris Ashley, Alec Baldwin, Andre Bishop, Scott Ellis, Doug Hughes, Judy Kaye, Andrew Leynse,* John Lithgow, Robert Moss, Brian Murray, Jack O'Brien, Neil Pepe, Theresa Rebeck, John Rando, Tim Sanford, AR Gurney,* Gordon Davidson*

2023 Creative Team

Directors: Violeta Picayo, victor cervantes jr., Julie Kramer
Stage Manager: Kat Sloan Garcia
Casting: Sujotta Pace
Production Design: Stephen Cedars
Stage Directions read by: Lulu Guzman

2023 National Adjudicator

César Alvarez

Special Thanks: Emily Dzioba, Stephen Cedars, Abbie Van Nostrand, Amy Rose Marsh, Garrett Anderson, Ben Izzo, Max Grossman, Michael Bulger, Aaron Malkin, Emily Morse, John Steber, Mark Orsini, Bonnie Davis, Michael Walkup, Michael Finkle, Luke Virkstis, Emma Feiwel, Sean DeMers, Lynn Rosen, Marvin González De León, Will Arbery, RJ Tolan, Andrew Knight, Taylor Williams, Karen Herskovitz, Katryn and Tim Barefield, Susan Buckley, Sofia Milonas, Sandra Graham, Julia Hansen, Bunni and Paul Copaken, Victoria Newhouse, Will Rucker, Jack Moore, Rachel Levens, Ella Andrew, Avi Amon, Brenda Withers, Thaddeus McCants, Adam Greenfield, James Wyrwicz, Alex Barnett, Jessica Lit, Ioana Preda Buburuzan, Emmanuel Wilson...and so many more!

---

* emeritus

FOREWORD

You are holding in your hands *Take Ten Volume IX*: a collection of five masterful short plays by the winners of Theater Masters' 2023 National MFA Playwrights Competition. This anthology includes work by MFA playwrights from Carnegie Mellon University, Hunter College, New York University, UCLA, and UT Austin.

These ten-minute plays explode with humor, heartbreak, and surprising theatricality as they confront larger-than-life themes like mental health, climate disaster, family conflict, and fading friendship. The authors behind the texts are at the forefront of their field, and we're honored to have been able to meet them and their work at this early stage in their careers through these bold and beautiful new plays.

The National MFA Playwrights Competition and the Take Ten Festival were founded in 2007 in order to bridge the gap between academic training and professional careers for emerging playwrights. For the past 15+ years, Take Ten's professional development opportunities and partnership with Concord Theatricals have provided playwrights with a career-igniting entrance into the entertainment industry, while introducing their voices to the landscape of the American theater.

Take Ten 2023 was presented for the first time in a brand new way: live readings, enhanced with design. This format allowed our playwrights to make edits and bring in new pages up until show time. Lights and sound elements, expertly designed by Stephen Cedars, made it possible for audiences to experience the full potential of each play. Directors victor cervantes jr, Julie Kramer, and Violeta Picayo achieved brilliant staging and theatrical tricks on and off music stands. We are grateful to our friends at Playwrights Downtown for letting us take over their Robert Moss Theater for a week of experimentation and play.

Thank you to our donors, Board of Directors, artists, industry leaders, Theater Masters' Alumni, and our National Adjudicator César Alvarez, whose time and expertise helped to make Take Ten 2023 – our first in-person year since the global pandemic – possible.

And finally: thank you for picking up this anthology. We hope you'll be inspired to bring these plays to life on the stage once again.

Sincerely,

Emily Zemba, Take Ten Program Director

Vicky Hansen, Artistic Director

TABLE OF CONTENTS

Below by Malena Pennycook 1
big and small by DJ Hills................................... 15
de tal palo, tal astilla by jose sebastian alberdi 35
ONE HUNDRED BEES by Katie Kirk 53
That Was Fun by Chad Kaydo............................. 67

Below

Malena Pennycook

BELOW was first produced by Theater Masters in New York City on May 5th, 2023. The reading was directed by victor cervantes jr. The cast was as follows:

EVELYN . . . . Shayvawn Webster
ANARA . . . . N'yomi Allure

CHARACTERS

EVELYN – 20s, cousin to Anara.
ANARA – 30s, cousin to Evelyn.

SETTING

A submarine two thousand feet below Monterey Bay.

AUTHOR'S NOTE

A "/" signals an interruption and cues the start of the next line.

Thank you: Alex Shaw, Kirk Lynn, UT Cohort, ETW, Mishpocha South, Lars, my family.

1

(A submarine two thousand feet below Monterey. Darkness. A voice.)

EVELYN. This depth will make you go crazy. This depth will make you lose your mind. This depth will make it so you never wanna see light again. A lonely depth, a lovely depth. Two thousand feet below

ANARA. Evelyn. Eveyln. Saw the Medusa again last night. She was so fucking ugly. It was like someone wrapped a plastic bag around a child, pulled it tight and strangled her. Should I write that down?

EVELYN. No.

ANARA. Mk. Evelyn. Evelyn.

EVELYN. Mmmhm.

ANARA. Saw another last night. Didn't know its name. But it was black on the outside with red inside it – what's it called, when it glows?

EVELYN. Biolumi/nescent.

ANARA. Bioluminescent. Looked like someone went to the deli, got a sandwich in a plastic bag, spilled ketchup all over that bag and then left it drifting on the side of the road... Write that down?

EVELYN. No.

ANARA. Evelyn. Evelyn. Saw one more last night. Looked like a breast implant, you know, all fluberry, like someone put glow tape on a fake tit in all these mystic shapes and patterns and then the tit just went a walkin'.

EVELYN. They're jellyfish Anara. They *do* look like bags.

ANARA. They're the loneliest looking things I ever saw. No brain no spine. Locomote by inhaling and exhaling. They offend me.

EVELYN. The very sun could offend you if you thought about it long enough.

ANARA. True. Not an issue now though. How long's it been since we saw that ball o' flame?

EVELYN. Day twenty-one.

ANARA. The time's drifting.

EVELYN. Don't let it drift too far. / We've got a job to do.

ANARA. Scribble scribble scribble write write write.

EVELYN. Got to find the big one. Hope nothing bad's happened since I last saw it.

ANARA. You really love these ugly ass fishies, huh?

EVELYN. Love's got something to do with it. It's for science.

ANARA. OK it's for science. I'm gonna do whatever I like and if anybody asks me why I'm doing it I'm gonna say, "It's for science." Now that's a skip to the front of the line ride as many times as you want express pass. I'm gonna put my bare butt on a big poster and say THIS! THIS HERE IS FOR SCIENCE.

EVELYN. Girl, you just TALK.

ANARA. What else is there to do?

EVELYN. Almost sunrise. Shh here comes...

ANARA. Ooooo one UGLY motherfucker!

(A tiny jellyfish appears. It's bioluminescent and a barely shade of blue.)

It looks like two plastic bags had a kid and then that kid flunked out of regular school and then that kid flunked out of reform school and then finally that kid flunked out of the school where they send kids who flunk out of regular school and reform school and then that's this bag.

EVELYN. Bereo.

ANARA. Not hungry thank you.

EVELYN. Not Oreo, Bereo. Ctenophore, a midwater predator. Bereo doesn't have stinging tentacles for capturing prey, so it swallows them whole. It feeds exclusively on other jellyfish. Write this down write this down.

ANARA. You know what? I hate him.

EVELYN. Hush.

ANARA. Eating your friends. Imagine that.

EVELYN. Anara, you are reactive. You have got a rage-oriented / response.

ANARA. Your house burns down in a wildfire you're gonna have a rage-oriented response too. Shit – we're living inside of the mother's rage-oriented response right now!

EVELYN. Shhhhh! Here they / come.

ANARA. Here they come.

(Light! Sound! A flourish of commotion! It's vertical migration, baby. Hundreds of aquatic animals come blasting upwards in one dense pack. This is the largest synchronized animal movement on Earth. They pass Evelyn and Anara's submarine in a sudden rush and disappear. Through the rest of the scene, sea life slowly grazes by.)

I never get tired of watching that. What's that one?

EVELYN. Polaris. That thing lives only in colder water. I wonder what it's doing all the way out here. Hi Polaris.

ANARA. Good morning Polaris.

EVELYN. We've gotta write this down.

ANARA. Dear Monterey Bay Aquarium, thank you for this unpaid internship looking at jellyfish on the bottom of the ocean floor after I lost my whole livelihood to a California wildfire. It makes me feel so young. Love, Anara.

EVELYN. I thought you wanted to come down here.

ANARA. Didn't have anywhere else to go. Thought it'd feel like a vacation.

EVELYN. Does it?

ANARA. No. But it's better than sitting in a pile of ash.

EVELYN. Come on, write what you see.

ANARA. Don't you think the aquarium's gonna find out that I'm not a research assistant eventually?

EVELYN. Not if you take good notes they won't.

(They observe the sea life.)

ANARA. That one.

EVELYN. Glowing sucker octopus.

ANARA. Mhm I thought so. Ugly. That one.

EVELYN. Deep sea cucumber.

ANARA. Oh yeah? UGLY. That one.

EVELYN. That's a Spanish dancer. It kinda undulates and weaves around, see? That's why they call it that.

ANARA. Okay little ugly, go on.

EVELYN. Anara, you'd better be writing.

ANARA. Little Spanish dancer walking down the street

> *(Clap clap.)*

Didn't know what to do so she stopped in front of me she said.

> *(**ANARA** watches the Spanish dancer.)*

Hey girl do that thing do that thing and switch.

Hey girl do that thing do that thing and switch.

> *(**ANARA** repeats the Spanish dancer's movement.)*

WHO ELSE HAVE WE GOT?

EVELYN. Helmet jelly! Anara, write this down.

> *(**EVELYN** and **ANARA** play Little Sally Walker with a bunch of fishes.)*

ANARA. Little helmet jelly walking down the street.

> *(Clap clap.)*

Didn't know what to do so she stopped in front of me she said:

Hey girl do that thing do that thing and switch.

EVELYN. Anara please.

ANARA. Hey girl do that thing do that thing and switch.

Who have we got now?

EVELYN. That's a googly-eyed glass squid.

ANARA. Evelyn, there's no one down here.

EVELYN & ANARA. GOOGLY-EYED GLASS SQUID WALKING DOWN THE STREET.

> *(Clap clap.)*

EVELYN & ANARA. DIDN'T KNOW WHAT TO DO SO SHE STOPPED IN FRONT OF ME SHE SAID:

HEY GIRL DO THAT THING –

DO THAT THING AND SWITCH.

HEY GIRL DO THAT THING DO THAT THING AND…

> *(The Stygiomedusa, the world's largest jellyfish, passes.)*

ANARA. Wow. That's a giant.

EVELYN. That's the big one. Stygiomedusa.

ANARA. Does it dance?

EVELYN. No he does not.

ANARA. He?

EVELYN. That's the one I'm joining.

ANARA. Huh?

EVELYN. That's the one that's gonna carry my future.

ANARA. Cousin, what are you talking about?

EVELYN. This world is burning up. California's on fire and your house is gone. The Amazon's on fire and their houses are gone. Australia's on fire and all the birds' houses are gone. What do you do when there's too much fire? You get wet.

ANARA. Sorry… What?

EVELYN. Think about it. Life's not going to end – it's going to change. How are we gonna be ready to go back to the ocean? We've got to learn to breathe underwater. How do we learn to breathe underwater? We have to make love to the things that do.

ANARA. And I'm still like… Huh?

EVELYN. I've got to be with that jellyfish. It's for science.

ANARA. Oh shit... You mean my cousin's lost her mind and it's for science. I'd like to go back home now please. I said I'd like to go back home right now please.

EVELYN. What are you going to go back up to? The burnt? The world's changing too fast – we can't go over or around it. We've got to go through.

ANARA. This feels more like going under. You're already alive! You've just got to maintain!

EVELYN. I'm thinking about the on and on.

ANARA. The on and on?

EVELYN. And on and on and on and on. The forever – it's got things to do with me.

ANARA. Not like this!

EVELYN. Then like what? This is my way.

ANARA. Evelyn.

EVELYN. I've taught you how to get this submarine back. There's only one direction to point it and that's up. The aquarium will send a launch boat after that.

ANARA. You're moving too fast, you've got to think.

EVELYN. I've already thought. I'm done thinking.

ANARA. Why did you bring me down here? You needed someone to get this boat back up to shore?

I thought we were...

EVELYN. We are.

ANARA. How so?

EVELYN. We help each other carry on.

ANARA. You should have told me before.

EVELYN. I knew you wouldn't have anything to do with it.

ANARA. So you are going in there? To be with that?

EVELYN. Best case scenario is I climb into the walls of Stygio and swim out with the future in me.

ANARA. And the worst is that you die a terrible awful brutal electrocution boom shock to the heart kind of death.

EVELYN. Isn't that always one sorry possibility?

ANARA. Cousin.

EVELYN. I love you and I'm already gone. Live down here long enough and you start to let go of that kind of sense.

ANARA. When did you get to be this way?

EVELYN. When I looked around a little.

ANARA. I always thought it'd be easy to lose a mind.

EVELYN. Just a little bit of effort and a short amount of time.

Don't cry.

ANARA. I'm not. I love you.

EVELYN. I'm gone.

ANARA. I love you.

EVELYN. I'm gone.

2

> *(Submarine. **ANARA** sleeps. **EVELYN** is in the control room.)*
>
> *(The big one approaches – a Stygiomedusa. Streams and streams of silky flesh.)*

EVELYN. Hello big one.

Stygiomedusa.

I know you're there.

> *(Over the course of the following monologue, **EVELYN** slowly undresses to reveal a swimsuit.)*

Okay Evelyn, don't get scared now. What you're looking at is God. What you're looking at is a thing that can age forwards and backwards. What you're looking at is something that knows how to be immortal. Hello. Hello. You know what I find so sexy about immortality, big one? It's the quiet. You get so much more quiet than everybody else. People have been saying, how are you gonna give? To the future? This is how I give, this is my way. Big one, my cousin's been saying you look like a bag. But she's wrong. You look like protection to me. Silk ribbon protection with arms like electric cables. You're the strangest thing I've ever saw with my eyes. And the most pretty too. It's the strange that's got to save us now. Realities hanging on by such a thin thread, the only thing that makes sense is the strange down here below. That's what you've got to give to me, big one. That protective strange quiet that needs nothing but darkness. That's what's going to be able to live long. I'm going, I'm going. This is how I get my rest.

> *(**EVELYN** is in her swimsuit.)*

Cousin – don't get stuck on the way home.

(**EVELYN** *exits the submarine.*)

(She disappears.)

(An enormous electric shock.)

End of Play

big and small

DJ Hills

big and small was first produced by Theater Masters in New York City on May 5th, 2023. The reading was directed by victor cervantes jr. The cast was as follows:

JP (13). . . . . Katherine Benitez
JP (19). . . . . N'yomi Allure
JP (25) . . . . Sushma Saha
TERI (32) . . . . Layla Khoshnoudi
TERI (38) . . . . Pooya Mohseni
TERI (44) . . . . Joslyn DeFreece

CHARACTERS

JP – 19
TERI – 38

and
JP – 25
TERI – 44

and
JP – 13
TERI – 32

SETTING

a driveway in a suburb in North Texas

TIME

evening

AUTHOR'S NOTES

On characters
all use she/her pronouns
all **JP**s and all **TERI**s are the same two characters
they are played by different actors
theatre is magic – they need not look identical

A note on levels
There is never an instance where **TERI** is not above **JP**
even when they are sitting **TERI** is still taller

(**JP**s *are lying on the driveway it is quiet here but never silent*)

(*lawnmower sounds continue throughout the play*)

(**TERI**s *enter*)

(**JP** *and* **TERI** *could be sisters*)

TERI (38).
waiting to catch a bus?

JP (19).
yeah so it can hit me

TERI (38).
—
don't joke about stuff like that

JP (13).
if you could take a bus anywhere – like anywhere – where would you go?

JP (19).
chill momma
buses don't even run out here

TERI (32).
i don't know baby
polk avenue?

JP (13).
mom –
be serious

TERI (32).
   i am –

TERI (38).
   mac is about to start a movie
   would you like to join us?

JP (19).
   no –

TERI (32).
   i need to get my nails done

JP (19).
   thank you

   (beat)

TERI (38).
   okay

   (she doesn't leave)

ALL TERIS.
   is dan mowing his lawn again?

   *(all **JP**s give an affirmative gesture that echoes through the years)*

   (maybe there's a sound)

   (maybe it's an eye roll)

TERI (38).
   i don't know how fast he thinks grass grows
   we're in the middle of a drought

JP (19).
   dan's an idiot

TERI (38).
   he taught – what?
   p.e.?

JP (19).
>   a.p. bio
>   he's still an idiot

TERI (38).
>   you failed his class didn't you?

JP (19).
>   because he's an idiot
>   i don't want to talk about dan anymore

TERI (38).
>   okay –
>   do you want to talk about erin –?

JP (19).
>   no mom
>   i don't

TERI (38).
>   at least she's spending the summer with her daddy so you won't have to see her
>   you two were so upset that you'd be apart over break but now look –

ALL TERIS.
>   one of god's little miracles

ALL JPS.
>   fuck god

TERI (44).
>   jp –

JP (25).
>   what?

TERI (44).
>   i don't know – it seems – i don't know –

ALL TERIS.
>   don't fuck god
>   don't fuck anyone

JP (19).
(laughs) mom –

JP (13).
(laughing) don't be weird –

TERI (44).
i just –

ALL TERIS.
i don't want you to ever be –
heartbroken –

(the levels change)

JP (19).
that's stupid

TERI (38).
why?

JP (13).
i'm not having sex momma

JP (25).
it's too late for that –

JP (19).
of course i'm going to be heartbroken
that's like
a fact of life

TERI (38).
(so terribly sincere:) baby i wish it never had to be

JP (13).
if you could take a bus anywhere –
like away from here –
where would you go?

TERI (32).
antarctica

JP (13).
> *(laughs)* you don't even know how to swim

TERI (32).
> i know other things

> *(lights dim)*

> *(the sun is setting)*

JP (25).
> hot today
> even for texas
> thought i was gonna drown in my own sweat
> i didn't think i could ever miss this kind of heat
> do you ever feel like that?

TERI (44).
> a lady doesn't sweat

JP (25).
> shut up
> i've seen you sweat

TERI (44).
> i was *glistening* –

ALL JPS.
> do you remember when erin and i helped you in the garden

JP (25).
> when we were small?

JP (13).
> i was thinking today –

JP (19).
> we made such a mess – trampling through the dirt –

ALL TERIS.
> i remember

JP (19).
(*realizing:*) we must have ruined everything

TERI (38).
(*shrugs*) you were having fun

JP (19).
but you –
were you pissed?
you must have *hated* us

TERI (38).
some days i did some days i didn't
(*laughs*) they were just flowers jp

JP (19).
yeah but they were –
i mean –
you *love* your flowers –

TERI (38).
i love you more

JP (19).
mom – stop –
you –
i'm trying to –

TERI (38).
jp you don't have to –

ALL JPS.
you put in all that work all that – time –

JP (19).
you should have been able to plant fucking i don't know hydrangeas without little kid toes smushing them all

TERI (38).
they were phlox

JP (19).
mom –

TERI (38).
>i don't know what you want me to say jp
>it is what it is
>when you have a kid you sort of give up some things

JP (19).
>like phlox?

TERI (38).
>like –
>–
>yes
>like phlox

JP (13).
>give me a real answer:
>if you could take a bus anywhere
>where would you go?

TERI (44).
>i'll cut you some before you go back
>maybe you can plant your own

JP (25).
>i don't need flowers momma

TERI (44).
>phlox grows well in california –
>even up north

JP (25).
>i promise –
>i'll just kill them

JP (19).
>i gave up prom for erin

TERI (38).
>i know

JP (19).
>i was so excited to go
>she knew i was excited

JP (19).
> i should've gone anyway
> –
> i hate her mom

TERI (38).
> that's okay
> i hate her too

>> (**JP** *laughs*)

JP (19).
> you've always hated her

TERI (38).
> not – *always* –

JP (19).
> well you hated cristi

TERI (38).
> because cristi's a bitch

JP (19).
> like mother like daughter

TERI (38).
> i hope so

>> (*she pulls* **JP** *into her*)

>> (*a seated hug*)

>> (**JP** *rests her head on* **TERI**)

JP (19).
> i hate that it's never quiet here

TERI (32).
> you tell me
> where do you wanna go?

TERI (38).
> honey this is about as quiet as it can get

JP (13).
austin

TERI (32).
it'll be loud in austin

JP (19).
no but i mean –
i mean – here –
here it's always the same kind of –
awful

TERI (38).
things are awful everywhere jp
i hate to tell you
you don't remember where we lived before mac

JP (19).
those places weren't *awful*
just
small
i hate it here

TERI (44).
i never expected you to stay here forever

JP (25).
but you would –
will –
stay here
forever?

TERI (44).
why not?
it's a beautiful place to settle down

JP (25).
(a mean laugh) "settle"

TERI (44).
what?

JP (25).
   nothing –

JP (13).
   but it'll be –
   different

JP (25).
   nothing –
   just –

TERI (32).
   different –?

JP (25).
   you know we fuck up a lot? like we fuck up and we fuck up and we take advantage of people's kindness and do-overs and one day someone somewhere – god or whoever – is gonna say *nope that's it you've made your decision now you have to deal with it*

TERI (44).
   jp i've never felt like i had to –
   deal with you

JP (13).
   yes!
   different –

JP (25).
   i know
   i know mom
   god this –
   this isn't about – *us* right now
   i'm talking –
   what i'm trying to say is –

JP (13).
   the world's so small here

TERI (44).
   i get it

JP (25).
>do you? because –
>because i kind of feel like you don't

JP (19).
>i think i might take a year off –

TERI (38).
>*(not meanly:)* no

JP (25).
>it's this *place* momma
>this – this stupid –
>like you can't even hear yourself think here!
>there's so much – so much *useless* noise –
>you can't think let alone make a decision –

TERI (38).
>berkeley is a big school jp
>who's to say you'll even see her?

JP (19).
>how would you know?
>you've never even been there!

TERI (44).
>what decision would you like me to make jp?

JP (25).
>i don't know! *anything* –
>as long as it's yours

TERI (32).
>the world will feel big soon enough
>just give it time

JP (13).
>but i don't want to

JP (19).
>i could take a gap year
>you know? try for ut austin or –

JP (19).
- join the peace corps –
build some houses –

TERI (38).
jp stop –
this – is a big decision –

JP (19).
i know

JP (13).
we could move way out into the desert
it's big there and quiet

TERI (32).
have you ever heard a coyote eat something?

JP (13).
no
have you?

TERI (32).
yes
and it is Not Quiet
(laughs) besides –

TERI (38).
so don't –
you don't need to –
shouldn't make choices –
because of a girl

TERI (32).
mac would never leave the suburbs

JP (19).
it's not about erin mom
it's about – i don't know – *life*
i didn't even want to go to california

TERI (38).
>but you did
>and you love it

JP (19).
>so? maybe i'll love south america
>or – i don't know
>zambia?
>new orleans?
>i haven't looked too much into anything yet but –

TERI (38).
>you're being –

JP (19).
>nineteen?

JP (13).
>we'll ditch him –
>you and me –
>who needs high school anyway?

JP (19).
>you made big decisions because of a girl when you were my age

JP (13).
>two tickets to the middle of nowhere please

TERI (38).
>that girl was *you*
>and that was different

JP (19).
>it doesn't matter

JP (25).
>nothing i say matters
>because – because you're not going *anywhere* – right?
>you're just going to sit here –

JP (25).
> with mac –
> forever –
> watching movies and growing *phlox* –

TERI (44).
> and i'm happy with that –

JP (25).
> *how?*
> how could *any of this* make you happy?
> i mean –

JP (19).	**JP (25).**
i wasted all that time	you wasted all that time
all those years	all those years
for what?	for what?
for her to leave me?	
–	
–	

i don't get any of that back

TERI (38).
> you're right jp
> you don't get any of it back
>
> > *(a moment)*
> >
> > *(a level change)*
> >
> > *(lawnmower sounds fade...)*
> >
> > *(to the rustle of the suburbs at night...)*

TERI (32).
> i want to change my answer:

TERI (44).
> when you were a baby i was so afraid of you drowning
> i gave you baths in the sink – even when you were too
> big for it – and then – one night – i had a dream that

i'd left a knife in the water and when i put you in the sink it split you – the sink filled with blood but you were so quiet – just content sort of – to be bleeding out in our kitchen sink – and i still dream about it sometimes –
your body splitting into pieces

> *(JPs are lying flat on the ground)*

> *(TERIs are above JPs)*

> *(they look at one another)*

TERI (32).
california
if i could –
you know i've never seen the ocean?
i bet it's big

> *(lights: purple)*

> *(sunset on the desert)*

> *(the distant howl of a coyote...)*

> *(silence)*

ALL JPS.
i'm sorry

> *(lights to black)*

End of Play

de tal palo, tal astilla

jose sebastian alberdi

de tal palo, tal astilla was first produced by Theater Masters in New York City on May 5th, 2023. The reading was directed by victor cervantes jr. The cast was as follows:

LUIS . . . . Andrew Rodriguez
MARISOL . . . . Florencia Cuenca
SOFÍA . . . . Angelica Santiago
JOSÉ . . . . Omar Chagall

CHARACTERS

LUIS – A queer teen, barely understands Spanish, not good at keeping secrets

MARISOL – Luis's mother, she loves him but is worried about Luis's future happiness

SOFÍA – Marisol's sister, recently divorced, she loves to get into the family gossip

JOSÉ – Marisol and Sofía's dad, Luis's grandfather, lives with Marisol and Luis

SETTING

Marisol's house

TIME

Sometime near our time, a little bit in the past, but only a little bit

AUTHOR'S NOTES

A commission from Teatro Chelsea for *El camino de cuentos encantadores*

Line breaks help break up thoughts
they don't necessarily indicate
rhythm
or
pauses

(We are in Marisol's home.)

*(**LUIS** and **JOSÉ** are sitting at the table.)*

*(**LUIS** is on his phone scrolling.)*

*(**JOSÉ** is listening to a mini radio tuned to a Spanish language channel or maybe he's reading a Spanish language newspaper. Both of them are in their own little very similar worlds.*)*

(A beat.)

*(**MARISOL** and **SOFÍA** enter.)*

SOFÍA. hola hola

JOSÉ. mija

cómo estás

SOFÍA. pues hay voy / papi

ya sabes

JOSÉ. así es hija /

qué bueno

LUIS. hi tía

MARISOL. párate y dale / un abrazo

SOFÍA. ay mari

don't worry

---

* A license to produce *de tal palo, tal astilla* does not include a performance license for any third-party or copyrighted recordings. Licensees should create their own.

SOFÍA. i know you love me

> (**SOFÍA** *kisses* **LUIS** *on the cheek.*)

and like oh my god by the way

i'm so proud of you

a high school graduate

my favorite nephew

and before i forget

it's not so much

i'm sorry for that

no one tells you how expensive divorce / is

but here

MARISOL. ya

por favor

es su graduación

LUIS. oh / you

thank you

SOFÍA. ya qué

MARISOL. no queremos hablar de tu divorcio / hoy

> (**SOFÍA** *hands* **LUIS** *a Hallmark envelope from her purse, the name* **LUIS** *is written across the front.*)

SOFÍA. y por qué no

MARISOL. porque es / su día

JOSÉ. niñas

SOFÍA. you don't care if i talk about my divorce today right

LUIS. oh no

not at all

i don't / care

MARISOL. i care

it's a special day

my baby boy is all grown up

i don't want to talk about sad things

SOFÍA. but isn't this a sad thing

empty nest

college all that

MARISOL. i'll have papi to keep me company

and luis will visit

LUIS. mhmm

MARISOL. with a girlfriend i hope

SOFÍA. or three

MARISOL. cochina

no es como tom

SOFÍA. so do you like blondes / or

(**LUIS** *looks visibly uncomfortable. He descends into his phone world.*)

LUIS. i'm hungry

is the food coming / soon

MARISOL. they're probably busy today with all the graduations happening

SOFÍA. que ordenaron

MARISOL. ese lugar chino en la everett

no entiendo porque le gusta pero es su día

SOFÍA. teriyaki yummy

MARISOL. ajá exactamente

    teriyaki / yummy

SOFIA. wait so

    what are you looking for in a forever match luis /

    brunettes or

LUIS. um yeah

    i mean

    i don't know

    um

    and i mean

    hopefully the girls in college are more

    um

    prettier or um er

    than at my high school

    right

MARISOL. no one is good enough for mi luisito

SOFÍA. no that's smart luis

    don't make the same mistake i made

    tom and i were high school sweethearts

    look where it got us

    i think it's smart you're waiting for the right person /

    i know i should've

MARISOL. the right girl

JOSÉ. ay pero que obsesión con que luis encuentre novia /

    déjalo vivir

MARISOL. papi

es solo una conversación

JOSÉ. ya sé pero mari

MARISOL. qué

JOSÉ. ya hemos hablado de esto

a lo mejor no va a ser novia

también tenemos que estar preparados para eso

SOFÍA. qué va a ser

una escoba

MARISOL. ya

ya

hoy no quiero hablar de cosas tristes

JOSÉ. pero porque tristes

MARISOL. porque no quiero eso para mi hijo papi

LUIS.	**JOSÉ.**
okay	pero él
you're all talking too fast	él que quiere /
but i heard hijo	tu sabes
what are you guys talking / about	
SOFÍA.	**MARISOL.**
how handsome you look	ya papi

LUIS. yeah yeah

don't tell me

(A small beat.)

JOSÉ. tu tenías esa amiga de chica no

cómo se llamaba

MARISOL. papi / por favor

SOFÍA. blanca

JOSÉ. no /

no

MARISOL. no sí

JOSÉ. blanca

SOFÍA. sí

MARISOL. pero ya

otro tema / por favor

JOSÉ. pues sí okay

entonces esa blanca

nunca me voy a olvidar de ese día que tu mama te encontró besándote con blanquita

(**JOSÉ** *laughs.*)

MARISOL. ay papi era un juego y nada más

mami nos encontró jugando príncipes y princesas

SOFÍA. ajá

y tú eras el príncipe o que

JOSÉ. entonces por qué lloraste y lloraste y lloraste cuando transfirieron el trabajo de su papa cuando se tuvieron que mudar

MARISOL. porque era mi mejor amiga

por favor

no quiero pensar en blanca hoy

no he pensado en ella en años

SOFÍA. pues fue tu primer amor no

LUIS. that's / love

MARISOL. cállate sofía

tú qué sabes de amor

SOFÍA. que poca / mari

JOSÉ. niñas por / favor

LUIS. okay

seriously what are you all talking about

love

SOFÍA. we were just talking / about

MARISOL. sofía /

no

    (MARISOL tries to cover SOFÍA's mouth.)

SOFÍA. your mom's ex-girlfriend

MARISOL. sofía

LUIS. wait

what are you

my mom had / a girl

MARISOL. no no

she was a girl we both grew up with and i was her friend

te voy a matar

your aunt doesn't understand english

SOFÍA. oh shut up mari

our mom

your grandma

found your mom kissing our neighbor's daughter when she was younger

    (A beat.)

LUIS. what

MARISOL. sofía oh my god

LUIS. are you serious

MARISOL. it was just a game

we were acting

SOFÍA. sure

i doubt you'd let luis play that game / now

LUIS. hey now / why am i

MARISOL. i was the prince

LUIS. the prince

SOFÍA. and blanca was the princess

and the two of them would sit in their backyard castle and kiss and kiss and kiss probably / more

(**SOFÍA** *laughs.*)

MARISOL. that isn't funny sofía

papi no puedo creer que ésta es la historia en la que pensaste hoy

JOSÉ. solo quiero que luis sepa que el puede traer a esta casa a quien quiera

yo lo voy a querer igual

(*A small beat.*)

no tiene que ser difícil mari

MARISOL. no

tú no te acuerdas papi

cuando mami nos encontró gritó y gritó

y gritó y mami le dijo todo a la mamá de blanca

y blanca me dijo que ya no quería ser mi amiga

y que era mi culpa porque las niñas no se deben de besar

SOFÍA. en serio

MARISOL. yo fui la razón por la que su papa encontró otro trabajo

en otra ciudad

era para que su hija no me pudiera volver a ver

JOSÉ. nunca nos dijiste

MARISOL. pues así fue

LUIS. did you ever talk to her again

MARISOL. what

LUIS. this girl

SOFÍA. blanca

LUIS. wait isn't that just like

white

SOFÍA. yes

yes

LUIS. her name was white

MARISOL. it's a common name in spanish pochito

LUIS. weird

SOFÍA. it's not

MARISOL. i haven't talked to her luis

since

no

LUIS. is she why you and dad / stopped

MARISOL. no

no of course not

cómo crees

i loved your dad

we loved each other a lot

a lot a lot a lot

but we just

we got to a place

we couldn't stop

hurting each other

LUIS. oh

MARISOL. but also i don't know

maybe

i think /

no

but

LUIS.	**SOFÍA.**
what	qué

MARISOL. maybe you know

it played a part

that

maybe

some part of me

i don't know

always

with women

SOFÍA. oh my god mari

MARISOL. what

JOSÉ. qué pasa

SOFÍA. mari es lesbiana

MARISOL. ay por dios no soy lesbiana

ni lo mande dios

lesbiana no

pero digo sí

creo que pudiera / enamorarme

SOFÍA. pues eso es ser lesbiana mari

    (**MARISOL** *is silent, she looks a bit upset.*)

LUIS. mom

i think um

mom if you were

um

a lesbian

or like bi

queer

i would love you the same mom

okay

i would still love you

    (*A beat.*)

MARISOL. shouldn't i be saying that to you

LUIS. what

why / would

SOFÍA. ay dios mío luis / por favor

LUIS. what

MARISOL. luis

    i think what your aunt is trying to say

    and what your grandpa was actually saying earlier

    is that if you in the future bring home a

    not

    woman

LUIS. a not woman

    so like what

    a broom / or

MARISOL. no

    a man

    if you bring home a boy

    if you bring home a guy

    or whatever

    i will still love you

    and so will your grandpa

        *(**MARISOL** looks at **SOFÍA**.)*

    y tú qué

SOFÍA. oh yeah i would still love you luis

    obviously come on

    i think there's even a congratulatory rainbow on that card / i got you

    yay pride

LUIS. oh my god

well

um

thanks

i wasn't planning on

yet

but i guess

(A beat.)

thanks

i love you guys

MARISOL. we love you too

always

LUIS. eres muy buena mamá mari

MARISOL. a veces no siento / que

SOFÍA. are you kidding

your son's a star and that's all you

LUIS. hey

give me some credit too /

please

SOFÍA. no

JOSÉ. y mari

MARISOL. hmmm

JOSÉ. a mi no me importa

solo quiero que seas feliz

MARISOL. gracias papi

JOSÉ. y sofi

SOFÍA. mm

JOSÉ. de verdad

nunca me cayó bien tom

(**SOFÍA** *laughs.*)

SOFÍA. te quiero papi

(*Marisol's phone rings. She answers.*)

MARISOL. hello

JOSÉ. que suerte tengo

dos hijas / maravillosas

MARISOL. okay

great

SOFÍA. is it teriyaki / yummy

(**MARISOL** *nods.*)

LUIS. i'll get it

MARISOL. my son will be right down

(*She hangs up.*)

thank you

i love you

(**LUIS** *kisses his* **MOM** *on the cheek and hugs her hard. The hug lingers.*)

End of Play

ONE HUNDRED BEES

Katie Kirk

ONE HUNDRED BEES was first produced by Theater Masters in New York City on May 5th, 2023. The reading was directed by Violeta Picayo. The cast was as follows:

EL	Nora Kaye
EM	Jackie Rivera
ECK	Arielle Yoder

An early draft of *ONE HUNDRED BEES* received a workshop production in the Philip Chosky Theater (Pittsburgh, PA) as part of Carnegie Mellon University's twentieth annual PLAYGROUND Festival of Student-Produced Work on Saturday, December 10th, 2022. The performance was directed by Katie Mae Ryan. The lighting design was by Allison McSwain. The sound design was by Ang Zarrilli. The cast was as follows:

EL	Katie Mae Ryan
EM	Mo Cambron
ECK	Mackenzie Wrap

CHARACTERS

EL – Woman, any age, any race and ethnicity
EM – Nonbinary, any age, any race and ethnicity
ECK – Woman, any age, any race and ethnicity

SETTING

Some big faceless media conglomerate where they produce capital-C Content.

(Separate, but also:) A stage.

TIME

The modern age, in all its oversaturated glory.

AUTHOR'S NOTES

If possible, there should be some kind of wacky wordless upbeat music playing while all the "robot scenes" take place. (If the music can be sped up during the moments when the scenes go faster, that's even better.)

The characters don't consciously realize they're in a play, but – in the back of their minds, they might be half-aware of it.

The more patently absurd & pseudo-Brechtian the robot scenes are, the better.

Don't be afraid to get weird!

> (**EL** *shuffles onstage, faces the audience. From the second she enters, her movements and speech patterns should be robotic and over-exaggerated.*)

EL. I'm a normal person. I'm just like you. I love to BUY GOODS and WEAR MAKEUP and EAT CHEESEBURGER. But. I have a SECRET.

> (*Beat.*)

I'm –

> (*She is drowned out by the sound of a loud honking horn.*)
>
> (*Lights change.* **EL** *breaks out of "robot-pose" into something approximating a regular human stance.*)
>
> (**EM** *walks onstage, dressed sharply; they're in charge here.*)

EM. Fabulous.

> (*Beat.*)

Your performance is going to change lives.

> (**EL** *and* **EM** *shake hands.*)
>
> (**ECK** *walks onstage. She looks around anxiously until seeing* **EM**. **ECK** *immediately sprints over to them.*)

ECK. Is this the – I was told I could, could be cast, I might get a role –

EM. Of course. So. Why are you a good fit?

ECK. *(Clearly pre-prepared speech.)* Ever since I was six years old, I knew I wanted to act. I –

EM. Pass.

ECK. Acting – um...acting has helped me become more comfortable with myself. I owe my life to / acting –

EM. Pass.

ECK. ...I had a stutter as a child?! And – and, and the process of getting over that helped me realize I belonged / onstage –

EM. Nope.

ECK. Wha–?

EM. Joe Biden used that narrative. You can't steal a *president's* sob story.

ECK. Oh. Uh...how about – uh, how about, about –

(Silence for a moment. **ECK** *panics.)*

I have vaginismus?

EM. ...Go on...

ECK. *(Delighted.)* I have vaginismus!

*(***EM** *nods.)*

I have vaginismus! It's when you can't... Things can't really, go inside me. And um I feel this total obliterating shame, it's like – every time I'm with someone I have to do this song and dance about "Oh The Strap Might Not Go In," and I'm convinced she hates me. And then I panic and ghost her.

I thought dating women would fix me but, if anything now it's worse, and I, I – I'm so so fucking tired of not being normal. Even telling you this – it, I've never told this to anyone.

That's a lie. I told my therapist. She keeps – she keeps dismissing it?

> *(Beat.)*

I don't like my current therapist. She's not a very good therapist.

> *(Beat, suddenly perky.)*

...And THAT'S why you should cast me in your show!

EM. Great! You're hired.

> *(Beat.)*

Memorize this.

> *(**EM** hands **ECK** a sheet of paper.)*
>
> *(**ECK** looks at the paper for literally two seconds.)*

ECK. Memorized!

EM. Great. So you – you're gonna stand there next to her, and she's gonna say the lines, and you're gonna say the lines. Got it?

> *(**ECK** nods. The scene resets to the same tableau as the show's beginning, with **EL** onstage facing the audience in robot-mode.)*

EL. I'm a normal person. I'm just like you. I love to BUY GOODS and WEAR MAKEUP and EAT CHEESEBURGER. But. I have a SECRET.

> *(Beat.)*

I'm –

> *(She is drowned out by the sound of a loud honking horn.)*

(**ECK** *shuffles onstage in robot-mode. She also faces the audience, does not make eye contact with* **EL**.)

ECK. Hello. I am sad because I am different.

EL. Wow! I am also sad because I am different.

ECK. ...Would you. Like to be sad...together?

EL. Yes!

(*They slowly robot-shuffle next to each other until they're holding hands.*)

ECK. Wow. We are so happy!

EL. Yes!

(*They shuffle-turn to face each other, bend over, and kiss. It should be cartoonish: a bend at the waist so only their lips and nothing else touch. Maybe their lips don't even touch and they just say, like, "mwah."*)

(*Lights shift. They break from robot-mode and become human again.* **EM** *shakes their hands.*)

EM. That's great. This is great. Your work is going to. Change! Lives!

EL. My pleasure.

EM. Let's rehearse this one more time.

(*The same scene repeats, about twenty percent faster.* **ECK** *goes offstage;* **EL** *is once again onstage facing the audience.*)

(*Lights shift:* **EL** *enters robot-mode again.*)

EL. I'm a normal person. I'm just like you. I love to BUY GOODS and WEAR MAKEUP and EAT CHEESEBURGER. But. I have a SECRET.

(Beat.)

I'm –

(She is drowned out by the sound of a loud honking horn.)

*(**ECK** shuffles onstage in robot-mode. She also faces the audience, does not make eye contact with **EL**.)*

ECK. Hello. I am sad because I am different.

EL. Wow! I am also sad because I am different.

ECK. ...Would you. Like to be sad...together?

EL. Yes!

(They slowly robot-shuffle next to each other until they're holding hands.)

ECK. Wow. We are so happy!

EL. Yes!

(They shuffle-turn to face each other, bend over, and kiss. It should be cartoonish: a bend at the waist so only their lips and nothing else touch. Maybe their lips don't even touch and they just say, like, "mwah.")

*(Lights shift. They break from robot-mode and become human again. **EM** shakes their hands.)*

EM. That's great. This is great. Your work is going to. Change! Lives!

EL. My pleasure.

EM. Oh! While you're here, I've got this – this new piece about mental health? And I'd love you two to be a part of it.

ECK. Of course!

EL. Wow! What inspired this?

> (**EL** *and* **ECK** *blandly smile and nod through* **EM***'s entire monologue, clearly not taking it in.)*

EM. I...I spent my youth with the spectre of major depressive disorder in my back pocket. Like, my own personal Sword of Damocles. You know – in *The Rocky Horror Picture Show*, when Rocky comes to life and he immediately starts singing about how ooohhh the Sword of Damocles is hanging over his head and ohhh his life is a misery and such and so forth? So – when I was younger, I tried to write this, this bullshit naturalistic script about the family history.

Visited my sister, my twin, she...she wasn't doing well. She'd been a professional beekeeper, but she – hadn't gotten out of bed in like a week. And I walk into her house, and, just: bees. Must have been – at least one hundred bees. Flying around. I, seeing her... It felt like the bees were – a curse, some kind of shadow. But I grew up.

But I realized: no one *wants* that. They want to be inspired. They want simplicity. They want everything nicely wrapped in a box with a bow on top. So, like – why not give them what they want, y'know? It's easier this way.

> *(Silence for a couple seconds.)*

EL. I'm sorry, I didn't quite catch that?

EM. Oh yeah I'm – I'm just really passionate about representation! Ha ha!!

> (**EM** *hands out scripts to* **EL** *and* **ECK**.*)*

(EL and ECK look at the scripts for literally two seconds.)

EL & ECK. Memorized!

(EL and ECK enter robot-mode again. They start off not looking at each other, but shuffle until they are sort-of looking at each other while still facing the audience.)

ECK. Can I tell you something?

EL. Of course! You can tell me anything.

ECK. A Mental Health Problem runs in my family. But I'm in therapy now.

EL. Wow. You are SO brave.

ECK. Thank you. It means a lot to hear that.

EL. I bet you LOVE your therapist.

(Lights shift as ECK breaks from the robotic reality.)

ECK. Wait, w-what –

(Lights change back; ECK snaps back into it.)

EL. Did you know? If you are feeling anxious, you can visit **[name of the nearest counseling center]**.

ECK. Wow! This is so helpful. Thank you.

EL. I love mental health!

ECK. Me too!

(Lights shift. They break from robot-mode and become human again.)

(EM shakes their hands.)

EM. That's great. This is great. I think we are really Making A Difference here. Let's try one more time.

> (*The same scene repeats, about twenty percent faster. Lights shift:* **EL** *and* **ECK** *enter robot-mode again.*)

ECK. Can I tell you something?

EL. Of course! You can tell me anything.

ECK. A Mental Health Problem runs in my family. But I'm in therapy now.

EL. Wow. You are SO brave.

ECK. Thank you. It means a lot to hear that.

EL. I bet you LOVE your therapist.

ECK. (*Glitching.*) MY THERAPIST IS BEES! BUZZ BUZZ. SHE IS ONE HUNDRED BEES.

EL. (*Not acknowledging* **ECK**'s *break from script.*) Did you know? If you are feeling anxious, you can visit **[name of the nearest counseling center]**.

ECK. (*Robot-mode again.*) Wow! This is so helpful. Thank you.

EL. I love mental health!

ECK. Me too.

> (*Lights shift. They break from robot-mode and become human again.*)
>
> (**EM** *shakes their hands.*)

EM. That's great. This is great. I think we are really Making A Difference here. Let's try one more time.

> (*The scene repeats again, twenty percent faster than the last time. Lights shift:* **EL** *and* **ECK** *enter robot-mode again.*)

> (*As it repeats,* **EM** *starts dancing. The dance starts out measured, slow, relaxed, and then over the course of the scene becomes deranged. Full-body flailing.*)

ECK. Can I tell you something?

EL. Of course! You can tell me anything.

ECK. A Mental Health Problem runs in my family. But I'm in therapy now.

EL. Wow. You are SO brave.

ECK. Thank you. It means a lot to hear that.

EL. I bet you LOVE your therapist.

ECK. (*Fully glitching.*) MY THERAPIST IS BEES! BUZZ BUZZ. SHE IS ONE HUNDRED BEES. SHE LOOKS AT ME AND I – I FEEL LIKE I'M FAKING IT, LIKE I'M NOTHING, LIKE SHE'S GOING TO STING ME ON MY FACE, MY HANDS. I'M AFRAID I *AM* FAKING IT. I'M AFRAID I'M A PRODUCT FOR CONSUMPTION. And I – I, I d– d–

> (*Beat. Breathes in. Breaks robot-mode, speaks slower.*)

I don't know how to make the me that is me be the me you see.

> (*Brief silence. The scene picks up again, not quite as fast as before.*)

EL. …Did you know? If you are feeling anxious, you can visit **[name of the nearest counseling center]**.

ECK. (*Robot-mode again.*) Wow! This is so helpful. Thank you.

EL. I love mental health!

ECK. Me too.

*(Lights shift. **EM** keeps dancing. Unmoving, **ECK** and **EL** stare at the audience, faces frozen into rictus grins.)*

*(**EM** dances faster and faster. Lights flash for a moment. Everyone onstage collapses to the ground.)*

*(**EL** sits up and screams, a wordless howl. She stands shakily, the robotic spell broken. She stands up to face the audience, mirroring the tableau from the play's beginning.)*

EL. I'm a normal person? ...I'm – I'm just like you. I love to buy goods, and to wear makeup, and – and eat cheeseburger. But. But I have a secret.

(Beat.)

I'm / gay –

(Blackout.)

ROBOTIC FEMALE VOICE. *(Offstage.)* The allotted time for this piece has run out. Thank you for watching *ONE HUNDRED BEES*.

End of Play

That Was Fun

Chad Kaydo

THAT WAS FUN was first produced by Theater Masters in New York City on May 5th, 2023. The reading was directed by Julie Kramer The cast was as follows:

JUSTIN .... Jakeem Dante Powell
SAM/SAMUEL/SAMMY............................Ryan Spahn

CHARACTERS

JUSTIN – A gay guy, 20s–40s, any race.
SAM/SAMUEL/SAMMY – Some other gay guys, around the same age, any race.

SETTING

A cute coffee place, a cute bar, a cute coffee place.

AUTHOR'S NOTES

– denotes a break or jump in thought.
... denotes searching for the next word or idea.
[ ] denotes something implied or gestured but not spoken.

(**JUSTIN** *and* **SAM** *sit at a table with two teacups.*)

JUSTIN. *(To us, holding up a teacup.)* This is a teacup.

(To us, nodding to his **FRIEND**.*)*

This is Sam.

(Then: A cute coffee place. **SAM** *is mid-story, so loud all the surrounding tables can hear.* **JUSTIN** *is looking around, embarrassed, like "WTF why is he so loud?")*

SAM. So I'm just going with it – if he wants me to fuck his boyfriend, who am I to say no, right?

JUSTIN. Sure –

SAM. So I *do* – I walk to Crown Heights – and he likes it – the boyfriend – and the other one seems to like it too – you know, *watching* – they're like *moaning* and all that – you know, *ohhhhhh* and *ahhhhhh* and like "Oh, daddy, that's *good*, daddy." Meanwhile, they're *my* age. And I'm like "OK, thanks." But – you know – I guess it *was* good – they got what they wanted – so – *fine* –

JUSTIN. Did you...*like* them?

SAM. But then I get this *text* – from the *first* one – and he's like "Can you call me?"

JUSTIN. Uh oh.

SAM. And I'm like "Why?" And he's like "My boyfriend just tested positive for *gonorrhea*," and I'm like "Oh shit. Now I have *gonorrhea*."

JUSTIN. *(Concerned.)* Oooooo.

SAM. So I have to go to my doctor, like "I may have been exposed to *gonorrhea*" –

JUSTIN. Ouch.

SAM. And I didn't even think this guy was *that* cute – I thought his *boyfriend* was cute but you know, you play along, and then maybe you get *gonorrhea*.

JUSTIN. But it's easy to treat? Right?

SAM. But then I have to *wait* to see my doctor – like *three days* – while it might be like *growing inside me*.

JUSTIN. Eeek.

SAM. So then I do the test and he gives me the shot anyway, like while we wait for the results – which are *negative*, thank *god* – but the shot *hurt*, and it's like *why* am I even *doing* this, you know?

JUSTIN. Yeah –

SAM. It's like, you try to have a little fun, you try to *meet people*, and you end up getting tested for *gonorrhea*. And I don't have it – thank god – but still.

JUSTIN. Good.

SAM. Anyway. How are *you*? Do *you* have gonorrhea?

(A breath.)

JUSTIN. I don't think so.

SAM. Well that's good. It doesn't sound fun.

JUSTIN. Are you gonna see those guys again?

SAM. No. Once you text "*gonorrhea*," it feels like it's over. Have you seen the boys? Have you seen Robbie?

JUSTIN. *(With a touch of guilt.)* Oh. Uhhhh...we had brunch? Like a month ago?

SAM. He came to Brooklyn?

JUSTIN. The West Village.

SAM. Of course. Well *I* haven't seen him. Say hi to him, I guess. When you see him.

JUSTIN. Yeah. I mean – we don't – we just had brunch.

SAM. Are you seeing anyone?

JUSTIN. I mean – I went on *a date*. Last week? But – I don't know.

SAM. Who is he?

JUSTIN. Just a guy from…one of the apps?

SAM. Is he cute?

JUSTIN. Yeah? I think? I don't know –

SAM. Show me.

JAMI. I don't want to be on my phone –

SAM. Show me. Just *show me.*

JUSTIN. Let's just – are *you* seeing anyone? After the… gonorrhea guys?

SAM. No, I'm taking a break. I don't need to go back to my doctor with any *questions* for a while. Do you wanna – Are you seeing the new Meryl?

JUSTIN. …No?

SAM. Do you wanna go? I wanna go. Can you go Friday?

JUSTIN. I…I think I'm booked…

SAM. OK. I wanna see it opening night but I guess I can wait.

JUSTIN. No – you should go. Go ahead – don't wait –

SAM. I can wait – if you can go Saturday – or even next week –

JUSTIN. No, really. Don't wait for me.

(A breath.)

SAM. Do you not want to see it? No Meryl?

JUSTIN. No, I mean, I do. Eventually. But don't wait for me. See it.

SAM. OK. I'll see it.

(A breath.)

Are you sure? It's *Meryl*.

JUSTIN. I'm sorry – I – OK. No. So.

SAM. What?

JUSTIN. No, it's just –

(Taking a breath to settle himself.)

OK. This has been really fun. I'm glad that we… reconnected. And this has been really *nice*, you know? But I – I'm not sure – I'm not sure we're the best… friends for each other? Right now. I think I need…a break?

SAM. A break?

JUSTIN. Yeah?

SAM. From…me?

JUSTIN. No – I just think I need to be – you know – really…mindful? Of how I spend my time? And I'm trying to assess? I guess? The things I'm doing, and – I think I need a break. From this. From us…doing stuff. I'm sorry.

(A breath.)

SAM. So you're *breaking up* with me?

JUSTIN. I'm just trying to be really mindful –

SAM. Yeah, you said that. So you're *mindfully* breaking up with me?

JUSTIN. I mean –

SAM. We don't even see each other *that often.*

JUSTIN. I know –

SAM. Like we have tea every few months in the neighborhood and bitch about boys. Like you can't just *fake it* once in a while?

JUSTIN. I don't want to be *fake* –

SAM. Wow. OK. I guess we're not friends anymore.

JUSTIN. I mean, we can be friends? Like if we run into each other – I don't want it to be awkward.

SAM. *(Sarcastic.)* Oh – OK – *good*. Now it won't get *awkward*. Great. I guess if I run into you *on the street* with someone I'll say "Oh, that's my friend Justin, we don't actually talk, because he broke up with me *intentionally* over tea."

(**SAM** *stands up to leave.*)

Just so you know, this was never *that fun*. It was fun, but – you're not *that interesting*. This was mostly just *you* talking about whether or not you should do stuff *everyone* knows you should do – so – you know – I don't know if I'd throw away too many people in your – I don't know – purging or whatever. So.

Goodbye.

(To the next table.) He just broke up with me. My friend just broke up with me. Here. Over tea.

(To another table.) Yeah, *he* broke up with *me*.

JUSTIN. *(To us.)* So that...went well.

(**SAMUEL** *sits at the table.* **JUSTIN** *and* **SAMUEL** *have cocktails.*)

JUSTIN. *(To us, holding up his cocktail.)* This is a vodka soda.

(To us, nodding to his **FRIEND***.)* This is Samuel.

(Then: A cute bar.)

JUSTIN. But what if – I don't know.

SAMUEL. What?

JUSTIN. Like is it mean? Like we *were* friends.

SAMUEL. I thought you decided. And you *did* it.

JUSTIN. But did I? Like can I go back?

SAMUEL. You don't want to though.

JUSTIN. But now I feel bad. Like I abandoned him. Don't I owe him something?

SAMUEL. Why?

JUSTIN. Because you just – I don't know. You feel like when you're friends with someone you're going to *stay* friends with them, right?

SAMUEL. No. I stop being friends with people all the time.

JUSTIN. Why?

SAMUEL. You just do – you start a new job, or they stop dating your friend, or you just forget to text them.

JUSTIN. Yeah, but that's not – you didn't *decide* to do that.

SAMUEL. You *kinda* did.

JUSTIN. But it's not like…premeditated. You just get busy – you just don't have time.

SAMUEL. But you could *make* time.

JUSTIN. You can't *make* time. There's only so much time. You can't *make* more.

SAMUEL. I'm just saying, if you want to see someone, you can do that. So if you're not seeing them, maybe that means you don't really want to. You're still *responsible* for it happening.

JUSTIN. It just seems *meaner* to do it on purpose. And like – if you just *happen* to stop talking – you *both* stopped. It's not like one person *decided*.

SAMUEL. Maybe. Or maybe one person did decide. And they stopped texting. And the other person *thought* they both got busy.

JUSTIN. OK. Yeah. But...

(*A revelation.*)

Shit.

SAMUEL. What?

JUSTIN. I'm like trying to remember everyone that's happened with. Like did they *decide*? Did they break up with me and I didn't even *know*?

SAMUEL. But if you didn't notice, you probably didn't really care. You kinda did it too.

JUSTIN. But maybe I *did* care. Maybe I should have cared. Maybe I *would* have cared, if I had realized.

SAMUEL. I wouldn't worry about it.

JUSTIN. Maybe that's what happened with Nathan. I mean it was weird after we stopped... [having sex]. And then he started dating that guy – with that nose thing – but even before that – oh my god. Nathan *totally* dropped me. On purpose. He barely even responds to my DMs. I message him and he just *likes* the message. That's not a *response*.

(**JUSTIN** *gets out his phone and starts scrolling.*)

SAMUEL. What are you doing?

JUSTIN. I want to see our last texts.

SAMUEL. When was the last time you saw him?

JUSTIN. Like a year ago? Two years? I thought we were *friends*.

SAMUEL. Maybe you *were*. But then you weren't.

JUSTIN. But if we were really friends, we'd still be friends. And now I don't have anyone to see the new Meryl with.

SAMUEL. Yeah, I'm not doing that. That Meryl is not my Meryl.

(Then: A cute coffee place.)

JUSTIN. *(To us, holding up a teacup.)* This is a teacup.

*(To us, nodding to his **FRIEND**.)* This is Sammy.

(To us, holding up a pair of scissors.) This is a scissor.

SAMMY. A scissor?

JUSTIN. A scissor.

SAMMY. I thought it was "scissors." Like "Give me the scissors."

JUSTIN. I say "scissor."

SAMMY. Isn't "scissor" a verb? Not a noun?

JUSTIN. I say "scissor." "Cut" is a verb. "Sever" is a verb. A scissor is a thing that cuts or severs.

SAMMY. *("Whatever.")* OK.

(Moving on.) Did you see the new Meryl?

JUSTIN. Not yet.

SAMMY. Oh you *gotta* – you *gotta* – it's – I mean it's – like you know what you're getting, and it's not her *best* – but it's – you know, she does the big laugh and the thing where she tries not to cry and all the hand business like she's just *so* flustered she can't *help* crying. It's – it's all the things but it's – you gotta go. I went opening night – all the Brooklyn boys were there doing their thing – like laughing, but like *performatively* laughing, like "Oh, do *you* get why *I'm* laughing" –

JUSTIN. Fun.

SAMMY. So go. Go tonight.

JUSTIN. I have tentative plans with Tommy? I need to text him.

SAMMY. Go tomorrow.

JUSTIN. Yeah, maybe.

SAMMY. *Anyway* – guess what – I'm moving.

JUSTIN. What?

SAMMY. Yeah, I'm moving to Washington Heights.

JUSTIN. But you love your place. You love Fort Greene.

SAMMY. I love this place more. My friend has this gorgeous top-floor one-bedroom with this amazing skylight – it's like *flooded* with natural light – and I've always coveted it and he's moving in with his boyfriend in Harlem and he's giving it to me and I'm moving.

JUSTIN. Why isn't he keeping it?

SAMMY. It's not right for two people. There aren't enough closets, and the kitchen isn't big enough, but it's the perfect single person's apartment, and I'm the perfect single person.

JUSTIN. Wow. Congrats. So... I guess no more Brooklyn teas.

SAMMY. Yeah...

JUSTIN. It was like our thing, wasn't it?

SAMMY. Yeah, I guess it was. We did it once and then we kept doing it.

JUSTIN. Yeah. It was nice…?

(Is this the end? Neither will risk saying what he wants.)

SAMMY. Yeah…you can come to Washington Heights…?

JUSTIN. Yeah…totally. If you still want [to do it] …? You could [come here] …? Or we could [switch off] …? But I don't know if [you want to] …?

SAMMY. Yeah…

JUSTIN. *(A solution.) Or.* You could have tea with Phillip. Does he still live up there?

SAMMY. He does.

JUSTIN. Yeah. Great. That'll be fun. You two will have fun. 'Cause it's – it's a long way to come here – it's probably not worth – you know – and we – we'll still see each other around.

SAMMY. Totally.

JUSTIN. Yeah. Like at parties and shows and whatever. We'll see each other. And we'll catch up. And I'll still see your photos and we can send little heart-eye emojis…

SAMMY. …Yeah. OK. Yeah. Sure.

(A breath.)

JUSTIN. *(Playing it off, like no big deal.)* I'll see you around.

SAMMY. OK. Yeah.

JUSTIN. *(To us.)* And we did. And we do.

(Pretending it's fine.) And that's fine.

(Moving on.) And that's it.

End of Play

www.ingramcontent.com/pod-product-compliance
Lightning Source LLC
Chambersburg PA
CBHW072017290426
44109CB00018B/2270